THE

EFFECT

Principles That Produce
FAVOR, INCREASE & INFLUENCE

ED TUROSE

THE HEROES EFFECT

PRINCIPLES THAT PRODUCE FAVOR, INCREASE & INFLUENCE

© 2017 Ed Turose.

Printed in the USA

ISBN (Print Version): 978-0-9980161-0-8

ISBN (Kindle Version): 978-0-9980161-1-5

This book has been prepared for publication by Wendy K. Walters and Palm Tree Publications, a division of Palm Tree Productions.

www.palmtreeproductions.com | www.wendykwalters.com

To Contact the Author:

WWW.FOCUSLIFEINSTITUTE.COM
WWW.EDTUROSE.COM

CONTENTS

Do not go where the

path may lead,

go instead where there is

no path and leave a trail.

−RALPH WALDO EMERSON

1

CHAPTER ONE

FOCUSIZE

I have a vision to train up a new breed of leaders. Many professional sports teams, when they are not achieving at a high level of success, go back to reviewing the basics. I believe these six principles have been lost in our society in recent years. Working in Fortune 500 companies for over 35 years, I am seeing a change in specific behaviors that are affecting the area of relationship building that affect the levels of success.

I want to help you focus on integrating these six powerful principles but we all know we live in a world full of distractions. A person who develops a lifestyle of focus can achieve higher and greater levels of success! The decisions you make to implement these principles after you read this book will dramatically affect your life and your future!

I call this "focusize" which is the exercising of your ability to focus every day. In order to get in physical shape, you need to exercise every day doing exercises to get your body in shape you want to portray. The same goes for exercising your thoughts and actions by staying focused.

Let's begin by defining the word focus.

- directed attention (attend — to apply one's self, to apply the mind)

- a point of concentration; to bring or direct toward a common objective

As mentioned earlier, when you begin to daily direct your attention and apply your mind towards a common objective, you are focusizing, or exercising your ability to focus. You must begin to understand that staying focused every day is critical to your success. Most people are easily distracted and end up not achieving their goals or objectives.

According to Webster's Dictionary distract is described as:

- to turn aside: divert

- to draw or direct (as one's attention) to a different object or in different directions at the same time

- to stir up or confuse with conflicting emotions or motives

Dr. Kevin Elko, leading sports psychologist, says, "In order to stay focused you have got to keep the main thing the main thing." You cannot allow distractions, disturbances, or disruptions to come in and take you away from your main objective where you are keeping your focus.

Success is described as a favorable or desired outcome, attainment of wealth, favor, or eminence. Most people get caught up in the distractions and end up maintaining a mundane or average lifestyle feeling frustrated when they do not meet their goals or objectives.

In consistency lies the power for success!

If we can stay consistent by developing specific processes in our life and stay focused on these processes, success will follow us! So let's begin with the process of implementing these six powerful principles that can reshape your life and meet your results.

A person who develops

a lifestyle of focus can

achieve higher and

greater levels of success!

CHAPTER TWO

SUPERHEROES

*Be more concerned with your character than
your reputation, because your character is
what you really are, while your reputation
is merely what others think you are.*

—JOHN WOODEN

A superhero is a fictional character that has amazing powers. We live in a world that has a fantasy with superheroes. It seems that heroes provide us with confidence in uncertain times. The numbers are bearing out that trust and confidence are at an all-time low in all areas of society.

In the late 1930s and early 1940s comic books introduced superheroes beginning with characters like Superman and Batman. During World War II, they became literal stars branching out into books, television shows, and action figures. The first Action Comics was published in 1938, which was Superman. Most of us spent hours watching the old black and white TV shows of Superman saving the day. In 1941, the first female, Wonder Woman, was introduced. In the 1960s and 1970s TV shows began to feature Batman, Robin, and such evil villains such as the Penguin, the Joker and the Riddler. Eventually, many sequels followed, and now they have become the top grossing films in Hollywood. (Source: *Mania*)

The top box office movies that are grossing the highest profits are the ones which have a hero or heroes attached to the storyline. The Avengers, Iron Man, Batman, Spider-Man, Superman, and Captain America all are on the top list and the top 10 super hero movies have grossed over $3.6 billion dollars. (Source: *Box Office Mojo*)

Jacqueline Thursby, Professor of folklore and English education, believes that part of the reason for superhero popularity is that Americans like imaginative entertainment. "They enjoy the suspension of belief and excitement hero figures in films offer," Thursby said. "We like to see variant presentations of familiar heroes. That is why we don't get bored. It is fun and refreshing to find variety in the familiar." Thursby also believes that superheroes restore hope.

"Everyone, at some time or another, needs to be rescued," Thursby said. "It might be rescued from illness, loneliness, too much work, etc., and hero figures provide temporary escape." It seems that these superheroes have become our role models since they always come out on top.

However, when we try to look up to people in today's society such as sports figures, artists, musicians, politicians, or business leaders, we see both moral and ethical failure.

Every one of us has been born with specific gifts, talents and abilities, however, we each need to learn how to develop, nurture and mature in these three areas. Most people do nothing with their gift, or are functioning at a very low level in their gift.

In addition, we need to gain acquired skills. When you understand your gifts and begin to develop acquired skills, you will see promotion, favor and success.

When you understand

your gifts and begin to

develop acquired skills,

you will see promotion,

favor and success.

CHAPTER THREE

LACK OF LEADERSHIP

A startling 86 percent of respondents to the
Survey on the Global Agenda agree that we
have a leadership crisis in the world today.
Why would they say this? Perhaps because the
international community has largely failed to
address any major global issue in recent years.

—SHIZA SHAHID

The definition of a leader is a person who rules or guides or inspires others. I have seen both good and bad leaders in the past 35 years in Fortune 500 companies. There have been many articles written about leaders and leadership. Here are a few thoughts on great leaders from my career experience. Leaders employ the following traits:

HANDS-ON

Leaders who are willing to roll up their sleeves and offer their expertise, support and encouragement to their team will see more productive results. I have had leaders who say, "I pay you to make the decisions" ... and when you do not achieve the results all the blame goes on you. They never wanted to get involved and yet the outcome in most cases affected the entire team results. Leaders who are hands on, however, pull their weight to achieve the desired outcome. They motivate and move toward the goal.

A leader is one who knows the way,
goes the way, and shows the way.
—JOHN MAXWELL

Example is not the main thing in influencing
others, it is the only thing.
—ALBERT SCHWEITZER

UNITY

How can two walk together unless they agree? There is power in unity where one corporate voice, one vision, one unified body can make things happen and change the outcomes. Not only will the ride be smoother, but you usually arrive there more quickly when everyone is on the same page.

My opinion, my conviction, gains immensely
in strength and sureness the minute
a second mind has adopted it.
—NOVALIS

No one can whistle a symphony. It takes
an orchestra to play it together.
—H.E. LUCCICK

RELATIONSHIP

Many of us put many hours into our occupation and the family suffers. Those leaders that promote a family atmosphere will produce greater results. Great leaders know the people working for them as well as those in their personal lives—their spouse, children, family members. They implement specific things that are applicable to that family, making it more relational and creating a more productive environment.

When something is missing in your life,
it usually turns out to be someone.
—ROBERT BRAULT

Outstanding leaders go out of the the way to boost
the self-esteem of their personnel. If people believe in
themselves, it's amazing what they can accomplish.
—SAM WALTON

Become the kind of leader that people would follow
voluntarily; even if you had no title or position.
—BRIAN TRACY

ACCOUNTABILITY

Many individuals work independently and have never been challenged to submit to a higher authority to become accountable. Without accountability, there will be no order. The greatest successes I have encountered in my personal and professional life is when I was held accountable by someone greater than myself.

A body of men holding themselves accountable to nobody ought not to be trusted by anybody.

—THOMAS PAINE

Accountability breeds response-ability.

—STEPHEN COVEY

Accountability is the currency of success. Feedback is the breakfast of champions—providing you with both awareness and ideas for growth. Accountability is fuel for reaching your potential.

—WENDY K. WALTERS

RISK-TAKERS

Change is inevitable and is constant. Great leaders constantly look ahead and are willing to take a risk, even if it might end in failure. I recently heard a statement from a CEO of a large company that if his people do not make at least two mistakes per year then they are not doing their job effectively. The key is to learn from those mistakes and establish key learnings on an on-going basis. Key learnings are based on reviewing what has worked and what has not worked in a given time frame. Each area is then documented so you do not make the same mistakes again.

Only those who risk going too far can possibly find out how far one can go.

—T.S. ELIOT

You've got to go out on a limb sometimes because that's where the fruit is.

—WILL ROGERS

SENSITIVITY

People go through seasons of ups and downs and some are truly hurting. We need to be sensitive to people when they are going through these seasons since in most cases it has a tendency to affect their work productivity and results. For example, if a family is going through a divorce, a sickness, or loss of loved one, a manager needs to provide sympathy and understanding during these times.

Resolve to be tender with the young, compassionate with the aged, sympathetic with the striving, and tolerant of the weak and the wrong. Sometime in life you will have been all of these.

—LLOYD SHEARER

If we are to live together in peace, we must come to know each other better.

—LYNDON JOHNSON

OPEN TO NEW IDEAS

Great leaders allow all participants to share their ideas. Many times certain behavioral styles dominate and drive their own ideas and do not allow or forget to provide others the time to share in a group or personal setting. Nobody likes working for someone who thinks they know it all. Without an open forum to discuss and strategize new ideas, the environment of creativity gets stagnant.

Those who cannot change their minds
cannot change anything.
—GEORGE BERNARD SHAW

Your assumptions are your windows on
the world. Scrub them off every once in
a while, or the light won't come in.
—ISAAC ASIMOV

OVER-COMMUNICATE

This is one of the most frustrating areas that I hear from people while working within an organization or team concept. Leaders that over communicate will keep their team members engaged, meet specific deadlines and help each team member understand the expectations of the project tasks. Weekly updates will keep your team focused on achieving the corporate and personal goals and objectives.

Precision of communication is important, more important than ever, in our era of hair trigger balances, when a false or misunderstood word may create as much disaster as a sudden thoughtless act.

—JAMES THURBER

You can have brilliant ideas, but if you can't get them across, your ideas won't get you anywhere.

—LEE IACOCCA

SUPPORTIVE

Everyone needs support from their leader when they are struggling to achieve their goals and objectives. As mentioned before, great leaders will offer their support along with bringing other team members or peers to provide additional encouragement and assistance. One way to be supportive of the entire team is to share successes within the team that might help support some other.

Each person on a team is an extension of your leadership; if they feel empowered by you they will magnify your power to lead. Trust is a great force multiplier.

—TOM RIDGE

A good leader accepts your past, supports your present, and encourages your future.

—UNKNOWN

ACTIVE LISTENER

With the busyness of this age of technology, we sometimes react verses responding to a situation and fail to listen for the most accurate information. Many times as my team shares with me the information they are receiving from our customers, I always make sure they go back and ask more questions to acquire the best, accurate information. In addition, I always make sure as a leader I am listening to my team members to maintain a positive working environment.

Most people do not listen with the intent to understand; they listen with the intent to reply.
—STEPHEN R. COVEY

Listening is a magnetic and strange thing, a creative force. Those who listen to us are the ones we move toward. When we are listened to, it creates us, makes us unfold and expand.
—KARL A. MENNINGER

TEN TRAITS OF A GOOD LEADER

1. They are hands-on.

2. They foster unity.

3. They value relationship.

4. They practice accountability.

5. They are risk-takers.

6. They operate with sensitivity to others.

7. They are open to new ideas.

8. They over-communicate so they are understood.

9. They are supportive.

10. They are active listeners.

CHAPTER FOUR

THE HEROES PRINCIPLE

Webster's dictionary defines a hero as an illustrious warrior, a person admired for their great achievements and noble qualities or one who shows great courage.

THE HEROES PRINCIPLE

The HEROES Principle exudes specific character traits that can change your life as you begin to apply these principles into your daily routine. Essentially, these six virtues call upon us to do what is right and avoid what it wrong.

VIRTUE: an admirable quality or attribute.

Society in general has loss these valuable principles that need to be reestablished in our personal and professional lives. Great favor and success will be yours when you can focus on and incorporate these into your life.

H   HONOR

E   EXCELLENCE

R   RESPONSIBILITY

O   ORDER

E   EXPECTATION

S   SERVANTHOOD

 **HONOR**

The first virtue is that of honor. Equated with the highest degree of respect, mingled with awe, purposed for the dignity and character of another person, those who show honor radiate a good reputation, good quality or character as judged by other people, and uphold high moral standards of behavior.

Honor is remiss in today's society. Begin to honor others by giving them the respect and valuing them as who they are as a person instead of what they do, and the result will increase the building of positive relationships. Honor is the manner in how you treat others, especially those who are your elders and peers.

According to writer and scholar James Bowman in his new book, "Honor: A History," he seeks to show that throughout the 20th century honor has been largely "discredited" to the point where the "word doesn't seem to exist anymore."

We live in a world full of dishonor to those in authority; many even dishonor those with different personality styles or cultural backgrounds than their own. Although many of us have been dishonored in life, choose to stay focused on honoring individuals, and you will see how this character trait will serve you well in all you do in the details of your life.

There are many forms of dishonor in today's society. Examples include disrespecting parents, political leaders, and those in the military or the police officers that put their lives on the line to protect us. There is rampant gossiping and complaining about our managers in the workplace. If someone has a different personality than us, we cast them aside as not worthy to associate with us. Being unfaithful and in rebellion to those who are placed over you in the workplace or within an organization is dishonor.

No person was ever honored for what he received.
Honor has been the reward for what he gave.
—CALVIN COOLIDGE

EXAMPLES OF HONOR:

- When you about someone's difficult personal season, yet you did not gossip or broadcast it to others, that was honor.

- Verbally thanking emergency workers, police officers or military personnel for their service, and even paying for their meal when you notice them at a restaurant, that's honor.

- Focusing on the main speaker at an event, staying off of your phone/computer & giving them your complete attention, that's honor.

- When your boss comes to town to work with you, and you provide them with their favorite beverage upon arrival, that's honor.

- When you assist your manager with their bags and physically help them when needed, that's honor.

- When you stop what you're doing and give your attention to a mentally-challenged or person with special needs who wants to talk to you, that's honor.

- When you buy a gift for a friend just because they are special to you, that's honor.

- When you publically pay respect to the mentors or leaders that have changed and impacted your life, that's honor.

- When you go out to dinner with your friend or spouse, and you give them your undivided attention in an engaging conversation, that's honor.

- When everyone in your company is complaining and you continue to stay positive and joyful in the midst of uncertain times, that's honor.

Honor comes from a developed attitude within your heart; you were not born with honor. It comes from a determination that you are going to walk out the culture of honor every day. Being in the corporate world for many years, I have seen many individuals dishonor their managers, co-workers and peers. This resulted in the majority of them being fired, reprimanded and losing favor and influence within the workplace environment. Choose to develop the attitude of honor so that it becomes who you are from the inside out!

EXAMPLES OF HOW TO USE HONOR:

Position: Do you honor your position in your workplace? While others are complaining, you can control the atmosphere in your work environment by practicing honor. As you bring honor into this arena, you will see strife, conflict and disunity leave. This comes by taking a stand for honor. You must lead by example and become the positive light in a negative world.

Superiors: Do you honor the superiors and supervisors to whom you report? Do you respect their title and function? The greatest way to honor a peer or a superior in the workplace is to serve them. For example, if they have been given a specific title and function, such as President or Vice President, be sure to include that positional title as you introduce them to others.

Co-Workers: Do you honor your co-workers? Many people in the workplace are complainers, moaners, grumblers, faultfinders, backbiters and gossipers. What about you? You have to be careful that you do not allow yourself to join in with those who practice such things, who, in most cases, are there just to collect a paycheck. Passion in what you do rules! When you stay above the situation and keep a positive attitude, then favor and success will come your way. Change the subject when they begin griping about the latest change in the company. Or even better, pay them a compliment & see the environment completely change!

Sports: Within a team concept involving all types of sports how do you honor your teammates, coaches, referees, or your competitors? Many times as an athletic you have been given a platform to show forth your character traits. You can either stand out because of your honor, or you can be remembered for a person who lost their cool and dishonored their coach or competitors. Remember someone is always watching.

PERSONAL FOCUS

Spouse: Do you honor your spouse or girl or boy friend? It is amazing how many spouses dishonor each other even in a kidding manner with their words. Do you still open the door, walk with instead of in front of, or defer to them in even ordering a meal? If you have children, or expect to have them in the future, please be aware that your children will notice how you honor or dishonor each other. In fact, a culture of honor can be handed down to each succeeding generation. At the same time, it is true that dishonor can negatively affect future generations.

Friends/Children: Do you honor your friends or your children and make a big deal to praise their accomplishments? There is power in words that are full of honor. Most individuals who have not grown up in a culture of honor have low self-esteem. Make sure to minimize their weaknesses and honor their strengths.

Parents: Do you honor your mother and father? This comes with a great promise of long life. I now realize and regret that as rebellious teenager I hurt my parents with some of the things I said to them. When I got out on my own, I began to realize how much support they gave and how good I had it in those days. In their latter days, I apologized and made sure they knew how appreciative I was of their love for me.

Church: Do you honor your house of worship with your tithes, offerings, and alms? There is great blessing in honoring God with our time, talent and treasure in life.

A few simple ways to start honoring others is by using Sir and Ma'am in our conversations. It is honorable to call older people by Mr. or Mrs. If you begin to respect titles of people and honor and respect titles such as President, Dean, Principle, Pastor, Manager, Priest, and others, you will see them begin to treat you differently because you have honored them.

I warn you that when you start speaking like this you are going to see a quizzical look on people's faces? They may ask: "Why are you doing that?" "Is there an alternative motive?" "Are you just showing off?" When I say "Yes sir," I get looks from my peers that challenge me to quit. But, because I know it produces great results, I am making a stand to stay in a culture of honor. Let honor go before you and make the way for your success.

While working over 37 years in Fortune 500 companies, I saw a lot of dishonor and I made it a point that when I saw it I countered it with honor. If you allow dishonor to come into a company, team or organization, it will cause a confusion, resentment, offense and a critical attitude that can negatively affect the entire organization. We need to honor people first for who they are and their value as a person and secondly honor the position or title they have been assigned to. Just because someone has a different behavioral style or tendencies different from you does not make it right to criticize or cause dishonor in your personal or professional environments.

PRACTICAL APPLICATION

1. Begin to develop an attitude of honoring someone close to you such as a family member, friend, loved one, a boss or a mentor.

2. You can start by addressing people by their title or answering "yes sir" when asked to do a specific task. If you begin to honor others, you will see how they begin to honor you!

3. Please detail out an experience you have had with someone who has portrayed honor and explain how it has affected your life.

4. Have you ever been dishonored? How did it make you feel? What did you learn from it?

5. Does everything you do honor others? If we do not know how to honor our family and friends who are close to us, then how will we know how to honor associates or co-workers?

Please list two situations (individuals) that you need to focus on to restore relationship with them. The rewards of walking in the culture of honor are waiting to be revealed in your life.

1.

2.

EXCELLENCE

Excellence is doing something very good and to the best of your ability. Excellence is a choice; you were not born with it. Excellence is the privilege of a lifetime. Decide to wake up every day and choose to walk in excellence. To excel means to be first in rank, above average, beyond the norm. Excellence is pouring out and demonstrating your best with what you have.

> *The quality of a person's life is in direct proportion*
> *to their commitment to excellence, regardless*
> *of their chosen field of endeavor.*
> —VINCE LOMBARDI

When you walk in excellence, you take ownership and 100% responsibility for your gifts and abilities. Most people are average and just do a job to get it done, but those who are HEROES, will do every job to the best of their ability and make sure it meets and exceeds the expectation of the person in charge.

Excellence will not tolerate unbelief, failure, procrastination, average, laziness, or the easy way out. Excellence is going the extra mile to do a better job than anyone else can do. Because the current generation has a history of doing only what they are told, it has become a major concern with employers. Be proactive when you see something that needs to be changed or fixed; step up with excellence and do it without being asked and you will speak volumes to an employer!

The heart of excellence is passion. Passion inspires people with energy, encouragement, and a positive environment. Excellence is alive with vision. When you get around people of excellence, you want to do something, go somewhere, and accomplish something enormous.

The reason why productivity is down in many companies is due to so many distractions that affect our ability to concentrate, stay focused and do the very best we can in every situation.

In order to walk in an attitude of excellence in your schooling, job, family and every day circumstances, you need to put stop gaps in place. You need to control the amount of time and energy you put into areas that do not produce effective results. I call these areas time wasters and that includes the great distraction of social media. A person with excellence focuses their time, effort and energy on things that fill them up and produce results—not spending time in areas that drain them.

EXAMPLES OF EXCELLENCE:

- When you are asked to do a job within a certain timeframe and you meet that deadline, this is excellence.

- When you help a co-worker who is struggling with an assignment and you develop the skill set needed to complete the job, this is excellence.

- When you are working for a company and you proactively accomplish more than what they have asked you to do, this is excellence.

- When someone makes a special request for you to do a task within a specific timeframe and you do not procrastinate but get it in on time or earlier, this is excellence.

- When you ask for help with a specific task from co-workers and you freely collaborate together, this is excellence.

- When you walk into a restroom, see paper on the floor and you pick it up, this is excellence.

- When, without having been asked, you clean up after dinner, wipe down the table, put all the dishes away and leave no work for anyone else, this is excellence.

- Even though you might not value the traditional workplace rules in your company, but you comply with them, this is excellence.

- When you are getting ready to leave work and you see your boss still doing something and you ask him if he needs any help, this is excellence.

Be a yardstick of quality. Some people aren't used to an environment where excellence is expected.
—STEVE JOBS

EXAMPLES OF HOW TO USE EXCELLENCE:

<u>Tasks:</u> When asked to do a task, do you always do it with an attitude of excellence? If not, then something in your life needs to change so you can reap the benefits of favor and influence that exemplifies excellence.

<u>Response:</u> When asked to respond to an email or a request from an employer, peer, teacher or a person in a position equal to or over you, do you respond within 24 hours or sooner? Most people procrastinate and do not get things completed on time; the attitude of excellence, however, responds to requests immediately.

<u>Preparedness:</u> Do you show up early for a meeting, class or at church or are you the last one to arrive? Recently, I was at a meeting and we were on a bus waiting for one person to show up. He finally arrived 10 minutes late. His actions affected the entire day of activities. He was remembered for this long afterward. Excellence

shows up early! I want to be remembered as a person of excellence and excellence happens by your actions and planning well.

Leadership: If you have an expertise or experience in an area and you are asked if you can do the job, the best example of excellence is to step up and lead in that particular task.

Practice: When you are playing a sport, an instrument or if you are involved with any type of activity that requires practice, the best way to show forth excellence is to practice as if you are competing. The best of the best will stay after most people left the field, court, or arena and not put the time, effort or energy into a thorough system or routine that will make them great at what they do. This quality of excellence distinguishes itself higher than the average person and will be rewarded in great favor and influence.

MY EXPERIENCE WITH EXCELLENCE

While managing multiple sales teams in my workplace career and being involved in leadership roles in other organizations, I had an expectation that my team would produce everything they affected in the virtue of excellence. Most people are average and their work ethic shows that.

Right Management ran an online survey and discovered only 19% of people surveyed reported they were "satisfied" with their jobs. Another 16% said they were "somewhat satisfied." But the rest, nearly two-thirds of respondents, said they were not happy at work. 21% said they were only "somewhat unsatisfied" and 44% reported they were "unsatisfied." This attitude affects the virtue of excellence since most people do not want to be in their current job.

When managers or leaders are looking to promote someone, they are looking for a person that has a positive attitude and delivers all their tasks with excellence. You should never have to be told what to do if you see something that needs to be done staring you in the face. It can be fairly simple as every time I go into a men's bathroom and see paper all over the floor, I stop and pick it up before I leave. When in college working in a mill, painting houses, selling shoes in a retail store, cleaning toilets in the college fieldhouse or selling billion dollar brands for the Coca-Cola Company, I did it all in an attitude of excellence. Operating in this virtue will get you noticed by your managers, leaders, peers and parents and position you for success in both your personal professional life.

PERSONAL FOCUS

Describe a situation that you were involved with where excellence provided a positive result.

Some of the questions we need to ask ourselves to determine if we have an attitude of excellence are:

1. If I looked at my current schooling or job, can others describe me as one who portrays the posture of excellence? Do my grades, job responsibilities and work ethic reflect excellence?

2. Have you ever been told by a boss, peer or mentor that you did an excellent job in a specific task? Have you ever been promoted for doing an excellent job? Describe the experience.

3. Have you ever wondered why someone else got promoted over you and the reason why? Could it be they are at a higher level of excellence than you are? What do you need to change to include excellence or improve in excellence in your job or schooling?

PRACTICAL APPLICATION:

- Take inventory of your personal conduct or behavior and identify the areas that you need to change.

- Ask some close friends to help you identify a specific area where can grow in the area of excellence. You might be surprised at what you hear from them.

- Look for ways to improve situations everyday by adding excellence to the mix.

RESPONSIBILITY

Responsibility involves being the person who caused something to happen. It is fulfilling a duty or task that you are required or expected to do. It is fulfilling something that you should do because it is morally right. It is being willing to be held accountable for your actions.

To be a HERO, willingly practice both personal responsibility and accepting the responsibility to serve others. In this age of entitlement, those who walk in personal responsibility for their actions, words and deeds will see greater favor and increase in their lives.

The greatest day in your life and mine is when we take total responsibility for our attitudes. That's the day we truly grow up.
—JOHN C. MAXWELL

Assume personal responsibility for your life. This means you do not wait for something to come your way by luck or circumstance, but instead, you take the initiative. You respond to life's opportunities and challenges. Don't let others make choices for you. Take action and follow up to achieve your goals. Look in the mirror—you are 100% responsible for where you are today and where you can go tomorrow. Choose well!

I applied for a new position with a major company. Before I went to the interview, I visited over 50 stores, did a personal audit of the products they sold and recapped my findings. I handed that information in with my resume and also wore a suit and tie during the interview and I got the job. I took the responsibility to present myself FULLY prepared and it paid off.

EXAMPLES OF RESPONSIBILITY:

- Do you take action and step up in specific situations or tasks and take ownership? This is responsibility.

- Do you take ownership of your behavior and do you accept the consequences of your behavior? This is responsibility.

- When you make a poor choice, do you take ownership of it and accept the penalties or cost of your choices? This is responsibility.

- When you focus on your future, decide to eliminate distractions and reduce time wasters that do not produce any value, this is responsibility.

- When you move beyond your own needs and begin to help others who need your assistance, this is responsibility.

- When you manage your time and focus on your personal goals and objectives and make that your number one priority, this is responsibility.

HOW TO USE RESPONSIBILITY IN YOUR DAILY LIFE

When you start taking responsibility for your actions, people will notice and consequently begin to ask you to take on greater responsibility. This will provide you with greater rewards ahead.

Identify an area where you need to step up and take more responsibility. You will begin to see how others will compensate your actions.

Don't pass the blame! It is amazing to me how many people, when they have done something wrong in the workplace, are so quick to blame someone else. Be honest; if you have the responsibility, then take it to the fullest extent and make things right.

Do you pray for those who have responsibility over you? I remember I was with the President of my division of a major corporation and I approached him and said I am making a commitment to pray for wisdom and insight for the leadership team. He acknowledged that prayer and within the next five years the innovation that came from my division had a success rate of new product launches of over 90%! That is unheard of because most new items fail in the marketplace. In fact, these new items in my market did so well that I gained a leadership market share over my national competitor.

Within a team concept involving all types of sports, how do you take personal responsibility for your actions? Does your work ethic match or exceed the best players on the field? No matter what team you are on in your life, each person has a responsibility to fulfill the position, job description or tasks assigned to them. When personal responsibility is lacking in one person's actions, it can bring the whole team down. The results you achieve in life are based on the choices you have made and the actions you have taken in the area of personal responsibility. Choose well!

PERSONAL RESPONSIBILITY FOCUS

Start taking responsibility in a small thing and then work your way up to greater areas of responsibility. If you are unfaithful in a small matter, then you will be unfaithful in a larger, more important matter. Unfaithful in a little, then unfaithful in much. Those individuals who take on personal responsibility for their actions, and are faithful in the little they have, will ultimately be rulers over much.

When you begin to use what you have been given and use it well, then you will be given more and this will lead to abundance. However, I have seen when you are unfaithful, even what little responsibility you have will be taken from you and given to another who is willing to take personal responsibility. The more you take on, the more you will be required to live responsibly.

Do you have an entitlement attitude or one of personal responsibility? According to Webster's Dictionary, entitlement is the feeling or belief that you deserve to be given something (such as special privileges). Compare that to the definition of responsibility which is the state of being the person who caused something to happen. Which state of being do you operate in?

It is amazing to me the lack of personal responsibility that I have seen in current years. Recently, a person decided to quit their job. Instead of giving a 2 week notice, they texted the employer and told them they were quitting and would not be in the office on Monday morning.

A local university professor told me recently how a President of a company that interviewed students from this university was appalled from the response he got from a student who interviewed with him. He said the student sent the President a text message back thanking him for the interview with text abbreviations and did not even think about sending him a written letter, or following up with a phone call.

If you want to be a HERO who succeeds in life, start taking personal responsibility for your everyday actions. Don't wait for something to come your way by chance or circumstance, but personally take the initiative and respond to life's opportunities and challenges.

PRACTICAL APPLICATION:

- Start taking responsibility in a small thing and then work your way up to greater areas of responsibility. Remember, if you are unfaithful in a small matter, then you will be unfaithful in a larger more important matter.

- When you start taking responsibility for your actions people will notice and begin to ask you to take on greater responsibility which will provide you with greater rewards ahead. Be prepared for it!

- Identify an area where you need to step up and take more responsibility and you will begin to see how others will compensate your actions.

ORDER

The word order means to arrange or organize in a logical or regular way. It means peaceful or well-behaved. Have you ever been in a place that lacks order or discipline? It can become chaotic and ends up causing an atmosphere of strife. Nothing can harm a family, business or organization more than strife that may involve bitter interaction, violent conflict or dissension. Strife causes friction, disunity, and conflict.

In order to gain greater productivity in any arena, you must prevent people from creating and feeding an environment of strife. There are laws that govern our lives to keep society running effectively. Without law and order there would be chaos. It would be survival of the fittest and each for their own. An ordered life thrusts us into structure, safety, security, and peace. A root of strife can be pride. Pride walks in disorder, but humility is a virtue of order. Structuring an ordered life means acting the opposite way of those around you. For example, exuding humility where there is pride, remaining calm when there is chaos, or choosing integrity where there is dishonesty.

EXAMPLES OF ORDER

- When you submit yourself to your manager or boss and their culture or way of doing things, this is walking in order.

- When you see the possibility of a volatile situation you are involved with and you defuse it, not allowing any room for strife, this is order.

- When you behave wisely in situations with integrity and character, this is order.

- Personality conflicts cause a lot of disorder. When you blend your personality style to get in sync with others, this is order.

- When you honor the laws of the land and obey them, this is order.

- If you do your work or homework in a neat, clear, and timely manner, this is order.

- When things seem unstable and you are able to control your emotions and remain calm and peaceful, this is order.

- Being stable, constant and unwavering in the midst of chaos and strife is order.

- When dissention, discord and rebellion appear in your sphere of influence and you remain in unity, harmony and agreement, this is order.

- When you do things decently and correctly, this is order.

EXAMPLES OF HOW TO PRACTICE ORDER

There is a protocol in the professional arena. I submit myself to the proper order of leadership. I obey the protocol and the instruction of my leaders with the best of my ability without complaining or grumbling.

As mentioned before, we have the opportunity to maintain a calm, productive environment without strife. We need to be the peacekeepers and peacemakers to drive the proper order in the workplace.

Within a team concept or inside any sport, you always need to understand the protocol and stay in order and obedience to the leaders of your team. Individuals who go outside the box and try to accomplish more than what is expected, end up hurting the entire team simply because the expectation is to accomplish the goal together.

While playing college football as an outside linebacker, we had two aggressive middle linebackers who would constantly try to do too much and over run the play and miss a tackle. This led to the other teams' ability to move the ball down the field easily and quickly outscore us. Maybe that is why our record resulted in a 1-9 season.

Another example was in my business team. The financial manager was very upset with a regional manager who was not in order to the company's ways of doing business. Instead of him staying focused on his job and letting the regional manager's supervisor deal with him, his personal health began to regress and I had to remind him to stay in order and do his job the way it was intended.

PERSONAL FOCUS

Family: There must be order within your personal life. This includes your relationships with your spouse, your children, and your immediate family. The husband must take leadership within the family and there must be unity when making decisions between the husband and wife. How you raise your children and the time and energy you commit to them is critical in training up a culture filled with order.

Church/Organization: There must be order in relationships outside the home—including your religious and organizational ties. There is an order for those who lead and cover you in church and organizations. You must understand the proper government of the organization or church and submit to that set man or woman who provides the local vision. You must not backbite or criticize those who are over you because that is out of order. It will cause division within a church or an organization.

Business: A hero will operate within the laws that are set before him or her. There are policies and protocols that are set in place in organizations. Working for Fortune 500 companies for most of my life, I had to obey the companies' Codes of Conduct and annually sign the policy document that I would conduct myself within their code. There were specific rules outlining the responsibilities, practices, ethical and moral codes that the organization expected me to follow in conducting all my business affairs. This is proper order.

PRACTICAL APPLICATION:

- Is there anything in your life right now out of order? Please take personal inventory and identify any specific area(s) that you can reposition to bring order to your life.

- Look for ways to change the atmosphere in your school, job or at home. If someone is operating in strife, then look to offer harmony and peace.

EXPECTATION

Expectation is a belief and a strong hope that something will happen or is likely to happen. It is to anticipate or look forward to the coming or occurrence of something. Expectation is the mother of manifestation.

We live in a world that exudes a just "get-by" attitude that says being "average" is okay. In fact, the news media is saying that young people today will not attain the financial status that their parents were able to achieve. I do not believe that news report, do you?

High expectations are the key to everything.
—SAM WALTON

Joyce Meyer says that hope is favorable and confident expectation; it's an expectant attitude that something good is going to happen and things will work out, no matter what situation we're facing.

The kind of expectation I am talking about is the word hope. It is not wishing something positive is going to happen but believing it will happen and looking for it to be revealed. It is a hope based on earnest expectation. It is like a chicken stretching its neck out going after a bug! It is aggressive and knows that it will occur. This is the type of expectation you need to create in both your professional and personal life. Your expectation can guide your future.

Expectation is determined by a combination of your personal experiences, how you think about situations, and your cultural or social patterns. If you focus on the negatives of fear, depression, worry, doubt, unbelief, frustration, lack of confidence, and other factors, this will lead to a lack of expectations or false expectations. Based on economic conditions and world events, many people are now more pessimistic than optimistic. What choice are you going to make — choose well! Negative people will hinder your expectation, so leave that crowd!

EXAMPLES OF EXPECTATION

- When everyone says we can't and you say I can, *this is expectation.*

- Those who dig and find solutions live in a *world of expectation.*

- How many times have great inventors failed, yet got back up to believe they would find the answer, *this is expectation.*

- Your attitude and *expectation* will bring you through life's hardest situations and circumstances.

- When you truly believe in something, know it will benefit your life, and are willing to invest time and effort into it, *this is expectation.*

- A farmer who plows his field, plants a crop, and believes for a harvest, *this is expectation.* You can use this same analogy in whatever you sow your time, talent or treasure into; there will be a harvest back to you.

- When I know what the objectives and goals are in my professional or personal life and I do all I can to achieve these goals, I have an *expectation* of a reward in the end.

HOW TO WALK OUT EXPECTATION

When the economy goes down and recession hits, expectation withers among the masses. Based on behavioral styles, over 86% of the population is pessimistic. They do not expect any good thing to happen to them. What about you? Can you rise out of the pessimism and charge your expectation with optimism and excitement for the future?

Expectation is greater than just wishing something is going to happen. In order to begin to expect things, you have got to see them before they happen; this is called faith! It is amazing to me that when Apple announces that they are launching a new product, the consumers have a great expectation that the new technology will meet their needs and wants. There is a buzz everywhere about it and when you get your new iPhone everyone wants to see the new additions and it usually it meets the expectation of the buyer.

In the same manner of anticipation, you need to raise your level of expectation that you will be an over achiever and reach the levels of success that will meet your needs and desires.

Within a team concept involving all types of sports everyone has a high expectation in the beginning of a season but how do you keep your expectation at an elevated level when a star athletic gets hurt or a team that you were supposed to beat easily ends up with an upset over your team that was favored to win? We all believe in the next person up rule, but sometimes that skill set is below the star athlete's abilities. This is where the person who operates in the HEROES Principle can stand out and become a great leader. People on a team gravitate to a leader who has an optimistic attitude and is focused no matter what the circumstances are before them. In other words, circumstances will not dictate our outcome; we will rise above it and keep our expectation at an elevated level. As a leader in these types on instances, you will need to mentor, coach and even persuade others to stay in an attitude of expectation.

If you have ever been in a national sales meeting like I have with Uni-Lever or Coca-Cola there is a high level of expectation in the room. Whether starting a new job, college, or launching new products for a company, hope, expectation, confidence and optimism are expressed. As the CEO of the Focus Life Institute LLC, my expectation with our strategic development tools is to help this generation identify and eliminate distractions, fulfill their destiny and become positive change agents to influence society. Expectation is the mother of manifestation!

PRACTICAL APPLICATION:

- Please review your current personal goals. Maybe you have not set any goals. Please do so and raise the level of expectation to achieve these goals.

- Identify opportunities that can help you achieve these goals. Study and gain information that will help you begin to see that your expectation is high enough to achieve anything you desire.

- In a current situation where you are involved, how will you raise your expectation higher? Add some type of action step to increase your expectation for greater results.

SERVANTHOOD

A servant is one who performs duties to serve others. To serve means to give the service and respect due to (a superior) and to comply with the commands or demands of someone or something. It is amazing that some people just have a servant's heart. These individuals possess qualities that are driven by:

- a particular set of principles

- pure morals and ethics

- positive ideals and values

- optimistic attitudes and beliefs

The modern era of servant leadership began with an essay, "The Servant as Leader," written by Robert Greenleaf in 1970. In it, he said: "The servant leader is servant first ... It begins with the natural feeling that one wants to serve, to serve first. Then conscious choice brings one to aspire to lead ... (vs. one who is leader first...) ... The best test, and difficult to administer, is: Do those served grow as persons ... (and become) more likely themselves to become servants?"

There has been much talk in this day about entitlement, the feeling or belief that you deserve to be given something (such as special privileges). We have seen many individuals have an expectation to be served by the government, the upper class, big business, or some other source when, in fact, the greatest satisfaction and approval comes from serving others.

> *My fellow Americans, ask not what your country can*
> *do for you, ask what you can do for your country.*
> —JOHN F. KENNEDY

Robert Greenleaf also stated, "Caring for persons, the more able and the less able serving each other, is the rock upon which a good society is built."

In teams or sports, how do you serve others? If you are the starter do you help your understudy? If you are the second team do you serve the starter? Do you lead by example to serve others or do you walk in a prideful manner that expects others to serve you? As a leader, you need to lead by example of serving your coaches, teammates and staff personnel. Do not ask if something needs done just go do it and let others be encouraged by your acts of servanthood to all aspects within the team.

EXAMPLES OF SERVANTHOOD

- When you are working within a team and you see a better way to do something and you share that idea in humility and offer to help, *that is servanthood.*

- Acknowledging others based on who they are instead of what they do is *servanthood.*

- Many people we encounter on a daily basis are broken and hurting from the circumstances within their lives; just by offering a "thank you" or a "good job" is *servanthood.*

- Remember he that is greatest among you shall be your *servant.*

- Finding ways to improve your community is *servanthood.*

- Honoring, respecting and volunteering to help individuals based on their particular function (e.g. manager) in your personal and professional life is *servanthood.*

- By working with others, affecting your community and making it a better place to live is *servanthood.*

PERSONAL SERVANTHOOD

As we have therefore opportunity, let us do good unto all men and women. When you visit those in need, such as those less fortunate, the poor, orphans and widows in their affliction and need, this is a great way to serve.

How do you serve others? Do you have favorites? If you have a peer or manager who has a different personality style than you does that affects the way you serve them?

I have been known in my company as the one who serves. When my boss comes to town to work with me, I honor her and serve her. I pick her up on time at the airport, providing her with an ice cold bottle of water. I introduce her as Vice President to people we meet and make sure she gets the respect and honor due her. I choose to serve her and others. We live in a society that is all "about me" with daily selfies and spending more time adding friends to our social media outlets than making everlasting relationships to serve others. Servanthood is a choice.

According to an article in US News and World Report, Mark Snyder, a psychologist and head of the Center for the Study of the Individual and Society at the University of Minnesota, expresses that there are benefits to serving others—especially in volunteerism. "People who volunteer to serve others tend to have higher self-esteem, psychological well-being, and happiness," Snyder says. "All of these things go up as their feelings of social connectedness goes up, which in reality, it does. It also improves their health and even their longevity."

Most people say they value volunteering to serve others because it's "the right thing to do," as well as other altruistic reasons. But the strongest drivers of successful volunteers are actually more self-focused notes Allen Omoto, a professor of psychology at Claremont Graduate University in Claremont, Calif. There are five main reasons people volunteer, he says.

Three are "self-focused":

1. Understanding: the desire to learn new things and acquire knowledge.

2. Esteem enhancement: feeling better about yourself and finding greater stability in life.

3. Personal development: acquiring new skills, testing your capabilities, and stretching yourself.

Two are "other-focused":

1. Sense of community: making the world, or your piece of it, better.

2. Humanitarian values: serving and helping others, often with a strong religious component.

FOCUS AND SERVANTHOOD

I want you to identify your current focused lifestyle of how you are serving others. I have pinpointed three areas where most individuals are currently living when it comes to their ability to stay focused and serve others in their lives. Which one are you living in?

Sufficient Focus: individuals focused on just enough to get by without trying to improve or better themselves. The focus is living a daily life of being adequate, sustainable and living in just enough for themselves with little or no motivation to go to a higher level of achievement. I have enough for me and mine and no more.

Self-Focus: individuals who are living for their own personal interests or advantage. The focus is self-seeking, involves ego and self-serving where they will do anything to get ahead.

Servant Focus: individuals who are focused on helping others along with themselves to achieve their objectives and goals.

Examples: A friend of mine in Baltimore, MD, gives away a home every year. He invites young people from all over the U.S. to come to Baltimore and work for 2 weeks to refurbish a home and then they hand the keys over to the new owners. This volunteer event even has the mayor of the city attending and has affected the lives of hundreds of young people who come to serve a deserving family.

When I was in college, I spent 2 1/2 weeks in the towns of Jackson and Mendenhall, Mississippi helping out a ministry that provided services for people in their community. It taught me how to interact and serve others less fortunate than me and affected my life in making me more of a generous and sensitive person. My daughter was involved in our church mission trips to Latvia and Romania and it provided her with an opportunity to see how others less fortunate live and gave her a greater sense to help others back in America.

PRACTICAL APPLICATION:

- Identify a place where you can improve your community or offer some type of humanitarian value.

- Look at ways to serve others every day such as helping an older neighbor, children in your community, or outreach opportunities locally & abroad.

CHAPTER FIVE

FAVOR

There is a law in the earth called seed, time and harvest. What you sow is what you reap. When a farmer goes out and plants corn, he is not expecting wheat to come out of the ground. This principle basically means that what you sow will produce a harvest of like kind in its season. Examples might be when you sow service – you reap service. Sowing kindness reaps kindness.

When you begin to apply the HEROES principle, you will begin to experience influence, increase and favor in your life. Favor is approval, support, popularity or preference to a person or group. Favor makes you irresistible and attracts others to you. Favor takes you to the top of your sphere and makes you look good. When you see favor coming into your life, you begin to draw others to you. They want to be like you, hang around you and follow you.

Favor puts you on the front line and helps you fulfill your destiny. Favor does not come from mediocrity, being ordinary or lacking in excellence. Favor is a powerful force that will bring important people to you. Favor will cause people to seek you out so they can invest in your dreams. Their presence and assistance will help you become even more successful.

However, if you do not invest in yourself by improving your strengths and practicing the HEROES Effect Principles that you have learned, you will be like the main character from the movie Groundhog Day—living the same average life over and over again with the same mundane results. It's time for you to fulfill your assignment and begin to influence your sphere with these powerful principles that will encourage others and bring fulfillment to both your personal and professional life.

Favor in My First Job

While operating in these principles as a young man, I submitted my resume to Lever Brothers (Uni-Lever, the largest package goods company in the world) and was 1 of 120 applicants. As the interviewing process unfolded, I was using my servanthood examples to position me for this sales representative's job. It came down to myself and two others for the position. On the Friday before they announced who would have the position the following Monday, I felt so strongly that I had this position that I called the manager and told him I believe I was the right candidate for the position. He said there were two others they were considering. On Monday, I received the call and started my career!

A year later as I operated in the HEROES principles, I was asked to move to the Health and Beauty Care Division and turn that business around. I agreed and within 6 months I was promoted to the manager over one major market and within a year I took over an additional market. The management team saw something in me that was above average! Walking in these virtues was producing favor and increasing my value to the organization for the next 10 years.

Climbing My Mountain of Success

After 10 years with Uni-Lever, they had a buyout for the Health and Beauty Division and merged with another company. During that transition, they asked me to move to another state, but I felt my time with them had come to an end. I was asked to stay on through the summer and would be out of a position in September. During that time I interviewed with Coca-Cola Foods

Division (Coca-Cola North America) and was offered the account managers job starting in September with a +20% increase in my salary, plus all the benefits of the Coca-Cola Company!

During my first 8 years with Coca-Cola, I was given the opportunity to run my business, but there was a high level of turnover. As people moved in and out of the region, I had the responsibility of running the entire regional customer base and was responsible to train the next rep that would be hired. In one year, there was a vacancy in both my manager's and the other sales rep's position and I ran the entire region, making the volume and profit numbers. The VP for the Central Region came in and told me, "You can handle this until we get some new people in the positions because we know the principles you run within your business."

Maintain Your Principles and Integrity

During my 8th year with the Coca-Cola Company my division was losing market share and began to downsize certain areas of the country. I was called in and given a severance package and left the company. Because I was certified as a consultant in the DISC Behavioral System, I took an idea that I had to market and present these materials into high schools and colleges. I submitted my idea to a man who owned the company I was certified through and he challenged me to start this new venture using his materials and outsourced me for this project.

For the first year, I was not paid and had to call on colleges and universities trying to sell a new product to an existing market. I learned quickly that the educational market does not move as fast as Fortune 500 companies!

This was a process that I had to use the HEROES virtues in and within 1 ½ years I was able to secure 15 colleges and sold over $120,000 of products. As time passed, the man who owned the company did not fulfill his promises to me and after three years I knew there needed to be a change. I had the passion to help these students, but lacked the resources and commitment from this owner.

Within a month, I received a call from Coca-Cola and was asked to come back to the company after being away for over three years. My prior manager got moved to NYC and was looking for someone to manage my old territory with some additional markets and he thought of me! Why? I believe because he knew I operated in the HEROES principles. I was asked to fly to our company headquarters and they literally begged me to come back and run the regional markets. The Vice president said that he knew how I operated my prior territory and would give me my 8 years back as tenure within the Coca-Cola Company. These days if you are let go in a month, you typically lose your tenure.

You see how operating in these virtues can even reposition you and give you favor.

Maintain Your Passion

After being back with Coca-Cola for another 5 years, I began to write books and materials on how to focus, especially geared toward this younger generation with all the distractions that are available today through social media, games, texting etc. However, the passion to help students was still crying out inside of me. Most managers and leaders retire and go south or west to a golf course community and do not mentor or equip the next generation. I have a passion to help individuals identify and overcome distractions, pinpoint their personal assignments in life, fulfill their destiny to become positive change agents in society.

I started the Focus Life Institute and created my own set of tools and on-line resources to help individuals in the areas of creating a lifestyle of focus, matching career choices with their behavioral style, discovering what sphere of influence they would succeed in, providing soft skill training in areas such as communication, collaboration, conflict resolution, creativity, and offering instruction how to interview to secure your preferred job.

After 27 years with the Coca-Cola Company, I have retired and am giving my entire effort and energy into my next assignment in life with the Focus Life Institute. Recently, my business partner and I were flying back from the west coast after reviewing our materials with a university and a young woman sitting next to me heard our conversation about our strategic development tools.

She told me she was very interested in what we were discussing. She worked for Amazon and admitted that she was bored and did not have any personal fulfillment in her life. She was in her mid-late 20's and said that she wanted a greater sense of purpose for her life and this is why we created the Focus Life Institute to meet her need! Her response was that she has always gone after the money to find a job. After 5 years of seeking the financial gain, something was missing in her life. She suggested we focus our attention on leaders who will make a difference in their personal life, workplace or community. So after coming full circle back to Coca-Cola and finishing my career, the passion and drive I had 20 years ago is reviving itself in the Focus Life Institute and the HEROES Principle.

Never give up on your passion or dream, but realize that there is a process to go from your purpose to the possession of it. However, by operating in the virtues of the HEROES Principle, favor, increase and influence will follow you through your personal pathway to success. Please remember favor won't always come immediately. You have to put these principles in motion until it becomes a lifestyle. You must be willing to go through the process of development and maturation. You will be tested and tried in these principles to see if your heart is true, but the rewards of personal fulfillment and purpose are worth the journey.

CHAPTER SIX

PERSONAL EXAMPLES

I want to relate a few personal stories of how the HEROES principle worked in the real world. The first one is personal. The second one involves a relative, and the final one involves a close personal friend of mine.

Overcome Adversity:
A Personal Story

After spending many years with a major Fortune 500 company and receiving very favorable performance recaps, I hit a major distraction. There was a severe accident involving my son and my wife and I had to personally become his caregivers. During this time, this accident had me so focused on him that it affected every area of my life. I realized that he took preeminence, but I had to stay focused to maintain my job and my other family relationships.

The company I was working for had a grading system as follows:

- **5.0 (Best of Class)** – very few received this performance rating

- **4.0 (Above Standard)** – some were able to attain this

- **3.0 (Standard)** – you are doing your job effectively *(most received this grade)*

- **2.0 (Below Standard)**

- **1.0 (It gets ugly!)**

Under a previous manager, I was averaging 3.0 and 4.0 ratings in all 5 of my key areas of focus. I came under a new manager and our personalities were very different. Although his thought processes were not similar to mine, he was one of the best managers I had experienced in creating business processes that produce great results. Prior to my son's accident and during a visit to my area in the fall of that year, he graded me very highly, and we shared a great work experience. Six months later and after the accident, I was in the company HQ to receive my final review for the previous year. He asked me what kind of year I had. I told him it was a great year compared to my peers. I came in second in volume achievement and number one in financial management—a major focus area of the company.

My manager's response to me was that even though it was a good year for me, he did not like the way I got my results. Therefore, he rated my performance with three 3.0's, and two 1.0's. I was now on 90 days probation and would be terminated after 90 days if I did not make some changes.

Because he had not worked with me for over six months and the last meetings together were favorable, I was in shock! What should I do? How should I respond? Was I going to honor or dishonor him? I personally know the Vice President of the company and I thought about calling him to complain. I could call Human Resources and complain. I could defend myself and show him to be in the wrong. Or, I could shut up, remain focused and honor this manager in spite of how I felt about the situation.

I got counsel from those I could trust and decided not to defend myself to upper management and to get focused instead! I began to raise my expectation level and believe that I would not lose my job, but be redeemed!

I had to take personal responsibility on my assignments and for the next 90 days, I refocused my efforts on my business processes and the areas that I could improve. I had to provide weekly updates and communication follow-throughs in areas where he felt I needed to change and improve. Every recap I put together and turned in, I did so with excellence, according to my manager's requirements.

A former peer of mine was promoted and given the task of holding me accountable in making the necessary changes. He flat out told me that I would be terminated in the 90 days, and that he was there to see what I was doing and had to report back to my manager; one of the greatest areas where you can improve your focus is with accountability. I stayed in order of what my manager was asking me to complete and change without calling upon anyone to complain or to ask to defend my case. I kept focused with expectation that I would see a great result in the end of this challenge.

In my daily work time, I kept my attitude and responsibilities in order. I took ownership for what my manager deemed as wrong, made necessary changes and put the proper protocol and methods into alignment to follow through on what he expected of me.

After working with me for six weeks, my peer supervisor's conclusion was that I just needed a few tweaks in only one area and he reported back to my manager to change both 1.0 ratings back to 3.0. I worked hard for those 90 days and in the end I knew if I stayed focused, I would see a major turnaround. I served both my peer, who was working with me, and my manager. I wanted them to know I was committed to the success of the company, that I was willing to change and also knew how to execute the necessary changes.

After 90 days I stayed in expectation, honored the people over me, did my work with excellence and took personal responsibility. I knew what I was going to hear next – a "great job" endorsement from my manager. As I moved on to finish that year in managing my team, I did not take offence or hold a grudge toward my manager. I saw his gifting and strengths and began to serve his vision for the region. Consequently, I began to see my results improve to levels that I had never achieved before. You see, while applying these six powerful principles, I was experiencing increased results in my personal and professional life.

The following March I was in the National Sales Meeting in Las Vegas when they announced the winner of the Sales Manager of the Year award for the prior year. And guess what? That's right, my name was called and I was honored, along with my food broker, as the Manager and Broker of the Year! How could that be when I was on probation for 3 months? I became a HERO – I operated in all 6 of those powerful principles and saw an awesome return on the investment of these values.

I needed wisdom to stay focused on the task at hand and the end result was an unexpected reward. Since that time, this manager has moved on and he plays a vital leadership role in that company. To this day we have a great relationship. He had a way of getting things done differently, and I needed to focus my execution on his way of doing things. By doing so, I was rewarded – standing on a platform in front of hundreds of my peers as the Sales Manager of the Year!

Stay the Course – Don't Quit
A Relative's Story

My second story involves a relative of mine who was hired by a local marketing firm. After about six months, the President, whom I knew personally, told me he was going to let my relative go. Since I had known this relative all of his life and I saw the great potential in him, I asked the company President on what grounds he was going fire this young man. He came up with many reasons for his dismissal with some that did not add up.

His first reason was that my relative did not know how to write and formalize an email. I asked the President if someone ever sat down and showed him how to top line and bullet point an email response. He responded no. Secondly, he told me that he was not getting along with his boss—a manager who had a very controlling personality. I told the President that no one in the office gets along with this manager and the rumors were that many people were going to quit because of their style of management. I personally heard from some of the marketing reps that they needed more support from this manager, but they didn't accommodate the team.

I explained to the President that this young man has a great work ethic. He laughed and said that he did not think so. He told me that my relative does not stay past 5:15 PM in the office. I asked him what the hours of operation were and he said 8:00 AM to 5:00 PM. He said he expected this young man to stay until he left—around 7 PM. I asked him if he ever told the young man of that expectation. He responded no. He said that he should know better.

I stepped into this situation and asked the young man's father what he should do. He told me his advice to his son was to quit and move on. I told him that if he focused and made a few changes he would be able to save his job and gain the valuable experience he needed to further his career. I told his father that if this young man quit this job without making an effort to change and get focused, it would affect him in every job he took in the future. His father told me to take over. I coached this young man in the following: email writing, blending his personality with his boss and remembering to check with the President each day before he left the building to inquire if he needed him to do anything. I told him to honor the people that were placed over him and to make these changes with excellence.

I brought all the family members together and began to discuss how to change this situation and turn it around. I told my relative that he needed to take personal responsibility for his future as I coached and guided him along the way. I explained to him that he needed to stay in order, keep his mouth shut and go do his work. During this time other employees who did not like his boss were just leaving the company and badmouthing everybody involved. I told him to stay in proper order.

He began to lift up his expectation and understand that he had an assignment in the marketplace. This was just a test for him to overcome. He knew that what he was learning in this company was preparing him for something bigger. Don't blow your future by quitting because, if you stay the course and work through the issues, you, like him, will build a great testimony.

As he began to focus on these things and served both his immediate manger and the owner, his status in the organization began to change. Within two weeks he was moved under a different manager who was more personable and who began to mentor him. After a few months his former boss was terminated.

Within six months, he was promoted over the entire central and western business units and became one of the top marketing sales representatives. During the next 18 months, he was the first marketing rep ever promoted within the organization and was moved to California from the East.

After five years with the company, he was recognized as one of the top producers, loves the Californian lifestyle, and owns five surfboards! He eventually left that position for a National Sales Management role with another company, oversees the entire country in sales and marketing because he had the experience from this past job that opened the door to a greater future. Why? He got focused, stayed the course and implemented the six powerful principles that promoted him to a greater level of success. He is a HERO!

Keys to Promotion and Ownership
A Friend's Story

My final example is about my friend, Mark, who began working at a local floral shop when he was a teenager. The owner asked him if he had a desire to work in the back part of the store and learn how to design arrangements. He agreed to try his hand in that part of the business. He took personal responsibility and began to develop his gift. Soon after, he began to get noticed for the excellent arrangements that were showing up around town.

Eventually, he was called in by the other local florist who owned the second oldest flower shop in America. The multiple owners offered him a position and the he began to aggressively honor and serve the partners and especially the owner.

As the years went by most of the other owners passed away and the last one living was the owner. He asked my friend if he wanted to buy the shop because none of his children wanted to keep it going. My friend responded that he did not have the finances to buy the shop. The owner told him that he would give him a sum of money every year and that if he would give that sum back to the owner he would one day own the second oldest flower shop in America. Essentially, he was getting the flower shop for free because he was operating in the HEROES principle.

In the midst of this transition, the owner began to display some emotions that could have forced my friend to leave, but he continued to honor, serve, and operate in an orderly fashion with a spirit of excellence during the final years of the owner's life.

After the owner passed away, my friend went to the safe in the store and there was an insurance policy that paid off the debt of the floral shop to the owner's family, and my friend became the owner of the second oldest flower shop in America. His expectation was that if he served and honored this man and treated his business like his own, it would result in his role as partner. However, by applying the HEROES principle he became the owner, not just a partner, and he has a thriving business within the community that provides him with influence and stature.

The store has branched out, offering both flowers and giftware. It is prospering within the community. Recently, a competitive floral shop which had been operating for over 85 years, closed their floral department and all the business went to my friend's flower shop, doubling his annual revenue. What a success story of utilizing the HEROES principle! These HEROES principle enabled my friend to be given the second oldest flower shop in the United States and has elevated his sales to the degree that his store is ranked in the top 100 flower shops in America.

The HEROES Principle

Honor
Excellence
Responsibility
Order
Expectation
Servanthood

Walking in these qualities will

bring you favor and blessing.

You will have better results and

experience increased success.

CHAPTER SEVEN

The HEROES Effect Profile

In this chapter, we want you to take the HEROES Effect Profile to identify the 1-2 areas you need to work on to become a HERO. I want to challenge you to do a personal inventory of your life. In the six areas of the HEROES Principle, which ones do you feel confident already operate in your life? If so, ask some close friends, peers, or an accountability partner if they also feel that you operate in any of the specific areas. Identify and write down which of those six HEROES principles you already regularly display.

Please take the profile.

HEROES EFFECT PROFILE

Directions:

For each numbered statement and relative to the section definition provided, indicate your actual personal performance or participation level as follows: Please award each statement in this profile the points appropriate for you and according to the following scale regarding the identified quality or trait identified in the statement. Please be truthful in your response to each question.

0—Never, 1—Seldom, 2—Sometimes, 3—Usually, 4—Mostly, 5—All the Time

Honor- *the highest degree of respect, mingled with awe, for the dignity and character of another person.*

RANK 1-5

1. Unless it involves a close personal relationship, I use the person's title (Mr./Mrs./Dr./Pastor etc.) when addressing an individual.	
2. I am moved with pride/emotion for celebrated community, memorial, or heroic accomplishments.	
3. I honor the elderly and the opposite gender in speech and service.	

4. I respectfully obey the law and those in authority over me with an open demonstration of proper behavior in action, attitude, and speech.	
5. I openly express my gratitude and respect for deeds done for me or for others.	
Subtotal A	
Percentage *(Subtotal A divided by 25. Multiply by 100.)*	

Excellence- *the completion of performance of anything with superior quality of effort, workmanship, attitude or character.*

RANK 1-5

1. I must produce things assigned to me with excellence	
2. I expect excellence from others.	
3. I am concerned about how others view or use the final product/performance for which I am responsible.	
4. I endeavor to give my best effort every time.	
5. I admire excellence and articulate that admiration to the responsible person.	
Subtotal B	
Percentage *(Subtotal B divided by 25. Multiply by 100.)*	

Responsibility- *the expectation and obligation of being answerable or accountable for some outcome; having the ability to distinguish and choose between right and wrong in meaningful situations.*

RANK 1-5

1. I am willing to be held rightfully accountable—even for sub-standard outcomes when I've tried my best.	
2. I say something is wrong when I believe it is wrong and do not participate in endeavors I feel are wrong.	
3. I am an organized person and timely fulfill all obligations as assigned.	
4. I protect confidentiality with those who trust me for it and I never betray a trust committed to me.	
5. I am punctual in all appointments and an efficient effective time manager throughout my vocational/professional duties.	
Subtotal C	
Percentage (Subtotal C divided by 25. Multiply by 100.)	

Order- *to arrange or organize in a logical or regular way; being peaceful or well-behaved and respectful and submitted to approved authority.*

RANK 1-5

1. I am a logical thinker and act based upon logical reasoning.	
2. I am disciplined in the use of personal finances keeping a true positive balance to a personal budget based upon real numbers.	
3. I work submitted to the acceptable protocols and processes of my employer or personal businesses.	
4. I engage my personal/vocational/professional relationships by blending my personal desires in a way that honors the needs of others first.	
5. I strive for peaceful resolution of issues through negotiations, collaboration and compromise even if the outcome is less than what my personal ambitions would prefer.	
Subtotal D	
Percentage (Subtotal D divided by 25. Multiply by 100.)	

Expectation- *to believe or have strong hope that something will or will likely happen; to anticipate or look forward to the coming or occurrence of something.*

RANK 1-5

1. My attitude and outward countenance toward others is that my cup is half-full rather than half empty.	
2. When assigned a reasonable task, I have confidence that I will achieve the assigned end and will be affirmed for the accomplishment.	
3. When a supervisor expresses an objective, I am able to join with that objective readily and give myself to making it happen.	
4. I am able to hope for things believed in even though currently I am not able to see them.	
5. Pursuing a vision/goal/objective is exciting for me and I am willing to work for whatever time it takes to see that "thing" achieved.	
Subtotal E	
Percentage *(Subtotal E divided by 25. Multiply by 100.)*	

Servanthood- *one who gives service and respect due to (a superior) and to graciously comply with the commands or demands of someone or something.*

RANK 1-5

1. I naturally put the needs of others ahead of mine; I am willing to help without coercion by doing any level of participation in meeting that need.	
2. On the job, I am willing to help those under me succeed and I give a full effort to the tasks assigned by those over me.	
3. I enjoy and regularly enter in to volunteer efforts that benefit community and community service organizations.	
4. I give myself to the organizations I participate in with the attitude that "if it's going to be, it's up to me.	
5. Although I don't give to get, I do believe that there is a reward that comes to me because I serve.	
Subtotal F	
Percentage (Subtotal F divided by 25. Multiply by 100.)	

Enter and Add the Subtotals
(Not the Percentages)

Subtotal for Honor	
Subtotal for Excellence	
Subtotal for Responsibility	
Subtotal Order	
Subtotal Expectation	
Subtotal Servanthood	
Total Score	
Overall Percentage	
(Total Score Divided by 150. Multiply by 100.)	

The HEROES Rating Scale

Below 40% = I'm lacking a HERO status

50% - 60% = I'm interested in becoming a real HERO

60 % – 70% = I'm now preparing to be a HERO

70% - 80% = I'm gaining momentum to be a real HERO

80% - 90% = I'm about to graduate as a HERO

90 – 100% = I am a HERO to those around me

My Individual HEROES Rating

Enter your HEROES percentages in the appropriate column and create a bar graph by filling the spaces below your subtotals.

%	H	E	R	O	E	S
100%						
90%						
80%						
70%						
60%						
50%						
40%						
30%						
20%						
10%						
0%						

My Overall HEROES Rating

Create a bar graph by entering your overall total percentage and filling in the spaces to the left.

10%	20%	30%	40%	50%	60%	70%	80%	90%	100%

8

CHAPTER EIGHT

40 DAYS OF FOCUS

I want to challenge you to do a personal inventory of life. In these six areas, which ones do you feel confident that you already operate in? If so, ask some close friends, peers, or accountability partner if they feel the same way you do about a specific area.

What areas do you need to improve in? At the end of each of these six areas in the practical application section, you were asked to identify specific areas that you needed to work on to improve. I would suggest you take the next 40 days and begin to focus on one of these areas that you feel you need to improve on. You can make the change if you stay focused!

Let's begin to "FOCUSIZE" on the virtue that you feel has the greatest opportunity to improve within your life. By focusing on "one" of these every 40 days, you can begin to master all six areas within one year. Imagine the fruit of our labor that within one year great favor and blessing can begin to flow into your personal and professional life.

Here is an example of how you can take one area and focus on it for the next 40 days.

FOCUSIZE EXAMPLE:

40 Days of Focus   **Beginning Date:**_____

Area of Focus: HONOR

- **People or Task Focus Area:** Family members, peers, co-workers, or specific tasks.

- **Action Plan:** List specific areas you can focus on to make this change.

- **Weekly Recap:** List specific things you did during the day or week that made changes in your behavior.

FOCUSIZE EXAMPLE:

40 Days of Focus   **Beginning Date:**_____

Area of Focus: EXCELLENCE

- **People or Task Focus Area:**

  - **Professional:** Improve my work by providing my manager with more detailed information and finish my work on time.

  - **Personal:** Improve the appearance of the inside and the curb appeal of my house.

- **Action Plan:**

  - **Professional:** Begin to over communicate with my manager so I know deadlines and the expectations of my tasks.

  - **Personal:** Develop a weekly cleaning schedule to improve the appearance of my home.

- **Weekly Recap:**

  - **Week One:** Was able to turn in my project to my manager with two days to spare and cleaned the outside of my home by raking leaves, cutting grass and doing trim.

You can take the example listed previously and add six more weeks to the process to take you to 40 days of focus.

FOCUSIZE EXAMPLE:

It is now your turn to create a 40 days of focus process based on your greatest opportunity area within the six HEROES Principles. I would encourage you to document your 40 days of focus in a personal journal so as you can review the improvement in each of the six principles.

40 Days of Focus   **Beginning Date:**_____

Area of Focus: _____

- **People or Task Focus Area:**

    - **Professional:**

    - **Personal:**

- **Action Plan:**

  - **Professional:**

  - **Personal:**

- **Weekly Recap:**

  - **Week One:**

Continue this process for all the remaining weeks that total your 40 Days of Focus. I recommend you keep a journal of your successes and take note of your key learnings on each virtue throughout the 40 day process.

We are what we

repeatedly do.

Excellence then,

is not an act,

but a habit.

—ARISTOTLE

9

CHAPTER NINE

SUMMARY

The opportunity to walk in these six powerful virtues of the HEROES principle is now up to you. Each one of these areas can be applied by one key factor - YOUR choice! You choose to honor, serve and do everything in the spirit of excellence. You choose to take personal responsibility, walk in an orderly manner and live in a realm of expectation.

The HEROES principle has been proven throughout history. Those who operate in these virtues have been positively affected as they made the choice to function in them day in and day out.

Your life too will drastically change when you begin to operate in these principles. Before long, they will become second nature to you. You won't even have to think about doing something specific to be a HERO. It will become a commonplace principle in your life.

In the meantime, you will begin to notice those who do not operate in these principles. It will be so clear to you that you are going to have to share your personal testimony of how these virtues changed your life and how they can affect others in the same powerful and positive way.

The HEROES principle takes you to a higher level of living. Most people do not operate in these areas and literally do the opposite of these values. You, however, have been equipped and trained how to become a hero. Go become a hero to someone else and train them to go to a higher level so that they may enjoy life to the fullest!

BE A HERO TO SOMEONE TODAY!

MEET THE AUTHOR

ED TUROSE

Ed Turose has over 40 years of business experience as a people manager, trainer, and strategic planner for two Fortune 500 Companies, Uni-Lever and for 27 years with the Coca-Cola Company. His expertise involves marketing, training, consulting and strategic planning offering strategic business solutions that increases profitability, productivity and efficiency.

Ed Turose, CEO of The Focus Life Institute LLC, offers on-line, educational, strategic leadership training courses that are focused on equipping individuals to help them climb their mountain of success. Ed's passion is to help individuals identify and overcome distractions, pinpoint their personal assignment in life, fulfill their destiny and become positive change agents in society. Our development tools were created to impact, educate, enlighten, equip, and empower this generation to help individuals to achieve their personal and professional goals in life.

Resources
www.focuslifeinstitute.com

The strategic development tools available on-line include the following:

1. Focus on Personal Behavioral Style - This tool was created to help individuals understand what shapes their behavioral style via a Focus Behavioral Profile, a graph of your top styles, a complete understanding of the DISC behavioral styles and how to blend with others to improve communication and success.

2. Focused Lifestyle - This tool helps individuals create a lifestyle of focus and reviews the following: The Power of Focus which includes identifying and overcoming distractions, creating a focused environment, initiating where to put your effort and energy and focusing on execution and excellence.

3. Focused Vision – was created to help individuals prepare for their future and find life's direction. We

help you create your personal vision statement and then identify six core areas of focus:

   d. Passion - what fires you up

   e. Placement - 7 Cultural Spheres

   f. Planning - developing a Life Plan

   g. Purpose-why you exist

   h. Possibilities (eliminating distractions)

   i. Peak Performance - (creating objectives, goals, strategies and measures).

The end result is an action plan to achieve your dream and fulfill your destiny!

4. Focus on Career Planning - is a tool that provides focus into a career choice thus saving time and money for individuals searching for a future occupation.

   a. Personal analyst of the DISC Focus Behavioral Style profile

   b. Description of the 16 national career clusters including Tech Prep

   c. The tool matches your focus style with specific occupations in the 16 Career

Clusters that help you save time and money in your career choice.

d. How to gain real world experience so you can land that perfect job.

5. Focused Insights was created to help you gain an understanding of your personal strengths and then apply this information into improving soft skills needed in today's workplace environment:

   a. Communication

   b. Collaboration

   c. Conflict Resolution

   d. Confidence

   e. Creativity

   f. Character

6. Focus On Social Influence - there are 7 cultural spheres that affect society. These include education, government, business, media, family, religion and arts and entertainment. This tool and profile identifies what specific cultural sphere you are assigned to influence, includes examples of those who have influenced society and offers direction how to become a positive chain agent.

7. Focus on The HEROES Effect - The acronym for HEROES is Honor, Excellence, Responsibility, Order, Expectation and Servanthood which are virtues that have been absent in our society. Included is a HEROES Effect Profile that will help you to identify what virtue you need to improve on to produce, favor, increase and influence in both your personal and professional life.

8. Focus On Interviewing For Success - reviews how to interview successfully. This development tool provides the following information to help you secure the job you desire:

   a. Behavioral interview

   b. Get in sync with the interviewer

   c. How to develop the STAR application that gives you the edge in the interviewing process.

   d. STAR Technique S – Situation, T – Tactics., A – Actions, R – Results

How to Implement Our Tools

Our development tools can be implemented in a variety of difference venues listed below.

PERSONAL GROWTH

Investing in yourself to gain information on your personal values and enhance your skill set. Individuals can take the development tools on their own or with the help of a facilitator, parent or guardian.

EDUCATIONAL FOCUS

All Schools—High Schools, Homeschool, Colleges, Universities, Technical, and Bible Schools. Our tools will improve retention, save the student's time and money and get them focused on their future.

ORGANIZATIONS, CHURCHES, GROUPS

We suggest a 40 Days of Focus curriculum that links corporate vision with personal identity to advance the local goals, objectives and purpose.

40 DAYS OF FOCUS COURSES

We live in an age of distraction. Successful professionals get help to stay focused so they will enjoy greater levels of success. At the Focus Life Institute, we have created our strategic development tools to be implemented by those who want to see personal growth, but have a limited amount of time to improve their personal and professional lives. Each of our tools can be implemented for 40 Days and create results. We call this, "40 Days of Focus!"

The Focus Life Institute is an on-line, educational, strategic training curriculum that is focused on equipping millennials, working professionals, and others wanting to advance their personal growth and development to climb their mountain of success. Our development tools were created to educate, enlighten, equip, energize, and empower people to overcome personal distractions, create a lifestyle of focus, and achieve their destiny.

Each one of our strategic development tools is flexible enough to be used based on your time constraints. We have designated the following areas for personal growth and development that would include 2-3 different tools to help you achieve your goals and objectives to see greater results.

FOCUSLIFE INSTITUTE

I Am Distracted And Unfocused In Life

Area One: I am Distracted and Unfocused in Life

In this age of technology and social media distractions, recent studies confirm that attention spans are now under 8 seconds. Many people are trying to find their sense of purpose in life. Our strategic development tools will help you reduce the distractions you face and help increase your focus. We do this in three ways:

1. We address Personal Identity by how to identify your personal strengths, inspiring traits, and ideal environment.

2. We help in developing a personal vision statement, identifying passions, and creating a sense of purpose by crafting a life plan and set objective, goals and strategies.

3. We help create a lifestyle of focus by creating a focused environment and constructing ways to focus energy and effort.

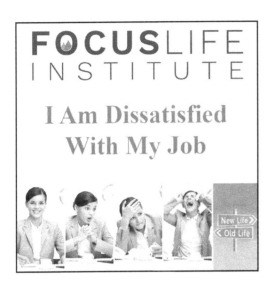

Area Two: I Am Dissatisfied With My Job

Many people are not satisfied with their job because there is no personal fulfillment or there is a lack of purpose. In fact, according to a new report by the Conference Board, a New York-based nonprofit research group, the majority of people—52.3%—are unhappy at work. According to Forbes, 75% of people stated that given the opportunity, they would have chosen a different career path for their lives.

This 40 Days of Focus module consists of three areas of focus :

1. Personal Identity which identifies your personal strengths, inspiring traits, and ideal environment.

2. Career Planning which matches your behavioral style with the 16 Career Clusters.

3. Interviewing For Success which provides interviewing techniques to secure your desired job.

Area Three: I Want To Advance My Career

Along with talent and abilities, many employers look for "soft skills" in order to promote and advance employees. Our program provides you with tools that improve soft skills such as communication, collaboration, conflict resolution, creativity, confidence, and character.

In addition, The HEROES Effect identifies six specific virtues to be effective in the workplace: Honor, Excellence, Responsibility, Order, Expectation, and Servanthood. Applying these virtues produces favor with managers and peers, increases opportunities for advancement, and expands influence.

This 40 Days of Focus module consists of three areas of emphasis:

1. Personal Identity

2. Focus Insights

3. The HEROES Effect

Area Four: I Need to Declare a Major Couse of Study

The National Center for Education reports that about 80% of students in the United States end up changing their major one to three times with an average cost of $10,000 per change. According to the CareerBuilder study, 47%—nearly half of students—are not employed within their major course of study. Only about 27% of college grads have a job related to their major according to the Federal Reserve Bank of New York.

This module will save you time and money as you get focused on your future. This 40 Days of Focus module consists of these three areas of focus:

1. Focus on Identify

2. Focus on Social Influence

3. Focus on Career Planning.

Our development tools can be customized in a 40 DAYS OF FOCUS Program and each of our modules include the following:

- On-Line E-Learning

- Individual Sessions

- Informative Videos

- PDFs and Personal Note-Taking Ability

- Exams Within Each Session

- Success Coaching Facilitator Guides

- Course Certificate

For more information, to review these courses, or to order our development tools please visit:

www.focuslifeinstitute.com

I don't care how much power, brilliance,
or energy you have—
if you don't harness it and
FOCUS
it on a specific target,
you are never going to accomplish
as much as your ability warrants.

—ZIG ZIGLAR

CONTACT INFORMATION

Website: www.focuslifeinstitute.com

Email: eturose@focuslifeinstitute.com